Charmed Lives

Congratulations on
winning the 2nd Prize
with the Undergraduate
Poetry Competition, 2012.

With warm wishes

Agnes Lehoczky

03.12.2012

The University of Sheffield

Acknowledgments

Ambit, Assent, Envoi, Interpreter's House, Iota, London Grip, Magma, The North, Other Poetry, Penniless Press, Seam, The SHOp, Smiths Knoll, Solitaire (Templar, 2007), Spotlight One, Staple.

'Rosie' won First Prize in the 2005 Ledbury Competition

'Mack' won Third Prize in the 2011 Strokestown International Competition

'From the Cabinet of Idioms' won Third Prize in the 2011 Larkin & East Riding Competition

'Wireless', 'Fugitive', 'Diplomacy' were finalists in the inaugural Manchester Prize 2008

Also by Mike Barlow:

Living on the Difference (Smith Doorstop, 2004)
Another Place (Salt, 2007)
Amicable Numbers (Templar, 2008)

Charmed Lives
Mike Barlow

Smith/Doorstop Books

Published 2012 by
Smith/Doorstop Books
The Poetry Business
Bank Street Arts
32-40 Bank Street
Sheffield S1 2DS
www.poetrybusiness.co.uk

ISBN 978-1-906613-52-5

British Library Cataloguing-in-Publication Data.
A catalogue record for this book is available from the
British Library.

Typeset by Utter
Printed by Charlesworth
Cover design by Utter
Cover image: The Logician's Sense of Herself by Mike Barlow

Smith/Doorstop Books is a member of Inpress,
www.inpressbooks.co.uk. Distributed by Central Books Ltd.,
99 Wallis Road, London E9 5LN.

The Poetry Business gratefully acknowledges the help of
Arts Council England.

Supported by
ARTS COUNCIL
ENGLAND

Contents

i.m. Pam and Morrey

Notes Towards Charmed Lives

for the beautiful
the modesty of a hellebore

for the thoughtful
a new idea oxidising in the air

for the deaf
the wing beat of a moth trapped in a cello

for the shy
the close attention of shadow

for the homeless
no false haven, no landlord's ransom

for the widower
the bridal white of crab-apple blossom

for the ambitious
a sneak preview of posterity

for the lost
a story to navigate by

Wireless

The voices are not here in the room.
Only my grandmother, reading
and patting her perm and looking up
from time to time to smile a papery smile
and my grandfather sucking at his pipe
or clearing his throat to spit on the fire,
and my mother sewing and not looking up.

The voices come from another world,
not this brown world with its bottlegreen
tasselled chenille table cover, but a world
of echoes and crackles, of happenings
not happening here, a world held
in a polished box with its grimace of light.
Stiff voices, cruel-to-be-kind voices,
voices with music and sometimes laughter,
though nothing sounds funny.

What the words say makes no sense at all.
But it's the voices I'll remember,
reaching into the room where no one speaks
and no one seems to listen. Theirs is a sound
I learn by heart – war memories:
making their own strange sense when finally
my father comes home with his terrible reticence.

Queues

I woke up inside my father's voice,
words beyond the grave:
switch that damned thing off.

We'd been watching Come Dancing.
I jabbed the standby button
and the screen blinked black,

sucking us through
the make-up room of memory
to lie doggo on a Dunkirk beach:

the soundtrack whine of stukas,
plumes sprouting from the sea,
queues of men inching out to the horizon.

Then there was music, a tinny
Greensleeves as an ice-cream van
came over the dunes. We joined a queue

for doubles with a flake and my father said
*When I was a boy they made me
learn the cello, what use was that?*

Well, you sent me away to school,
I replied, *to make a man of me.
I've refused to grow up since.*

My father reached up (he was shrinking
as we spoke) stroked my hand
the way he never did and in a voice

growing fainter and fainter explained
how you got the best sound holding the bow
with the wrist at the correct angle.

The Lifeboat

Already there were too many of us
and the war hadn't started yet.
If anyone had asked we'd have said
there was no room. Yet here she was,
all arms and legs, clambering on board
as if by right, knees and elbows
getting in the way whatever she did
to fold or arrange herself.

And her hair, a pre-Raphaelite mop,
bleached and auburn ropes bunched
and tossed as she bent to unpick
knots and tangles, oblivious to us all –
huddle of strangers in our lifeboat,
not rocking on the sea but secure
and made fast aboard the last ferry home,
its crammed companionways, crowded decks.
From time to time the bubble of chatter
burst into a hush as we caught each other
listening for the future sounds of war.

Had we been adrift and foundering
in The Channel, it might have been
'last in first overboard.' But I like to think
she'd have given us the slip, back-flip
and splash, that hair streaming kelp,
those legs elegant as she kicked out for France,
not believing in rumour, politics, anything
she hadn't seen for herself, believing only
in a lover she'd left to his fate in Normandy.

Last Minute Leave

They'd agreed to meet in the tea-shop
where once he'd talked so fast
she'd had to squeeze his hand to stop him.
This time words failed. Between them
a pot brewed, buttered scones cooled.
They listened to the landings on the wireless,
beaches where just hours away he'd jump.

He reached across to stroke her arm,
committing her flesh to memory.
She held his gaze as it clouded over.
They read their fortunes in the tea-leaves
and as they left he slipped her cup
with its pink rim and roses round the handle
between the buttons of his tunic.

Later, where the tea-shop stood
the sockets of wrecked rooms gaped,
joists stuck into space. But the cup, intact,
lay hidden in a field in Normandy
where in years to come
a farmer's son out rabbitting
would toss it in the air for target practice.

String Figures

One of us asks. He feigns deafness.
A son or daughter fetches a length of string,
ties a loop, places it across his hands,

a token gesture from the old rules
he still likes to play by. The muscles
round his mouth ease then, the austere scowl

folds to a jester's quizzical frown:
his party piece, a chance to reel in
the affections of a squabbling family.

He shuts his eyes, parts his hands
until the loop's strung taut, a simple cradle
to weave a story from.

We know it well, not for the words,
but the illustrations sleighted
from the shuttles of his fingers:

tallow candles, scissors, a tall chair and a ladder.
Grandchildren may lose the plot
but not the moment. Everybody claps.

He next makes thunderclouds and lightning,
an albatross, a man climbing a tree
to look down on his past.

Wrapped in its map his face wrinkles
as he shakes the net he's caught in,
knotted joints, string limbs.

A sudden deft flick and his startled look
stares back at us, straight through the open loop
for which there is no story yet.

Watching

after Per Petterson, Out Stealing Horses

I see him setting out the tools,
checking the ladder, wedging a rock
against the feet to stop it slipping.
Each time I face a job I'm not sure of,
like replacing roof slates or reglazing
a window smashed by a fallen birch,
this is what I do: I close my eyes
and picture my father, imagine
how he would have gone about it.
Or I'll go back to when I was fifteen,
watching him, unaware of everything
I was to learn from this man of forty,
about to step out of my life forever.

There's always a particular order,
the right sequence, first one thing
then another. I'll follow him as he fixes
cardboard behind the cracked pane,
chips away at brittle putty,
pulling the pins as he goes,
and with gloved hands works
the blades of glass loose, each task
a step in a ritual which,
performed in the right order unlocks
a secret I've known all along.

I watch his body moving from one step
to the next, unaware I'm there.
I've been doing it for fifty years now,
my mind's eye still fixed
on the movement and skills of a man
forever forty, and always the boy in me
embarrassed or impatient when I drop a chisel
or have to scrabble around for the hammer
with a mouth full of nails.

Masterpiece

Uncle Harold had a nicotine-stained moustache,
brown and yellow fingers and this party trick:
he'd peel his shirt off, wave it like Crusoe
at a passing ship, so everyone could clock
the Bayeux Tapestry tattooed round his torso.
The whip-round afterwards raked in cash
for a favourite charity some smart Alec
could usually be counted on to declare
suspect.
         My mother swore
he'd always been a sucker for a dare,
though my father put him on the back foot once
suggesting his car keys might be safer
with the police. *Nah*, he said, *I don't do stunts*,
and climbed into the silver Rover
he used to drive sedately as a chauffeur,
even cross-eyed drunk.
He died at 86, cheating at crib.
After the service with its good old-fashioned hymns,
the Battle of Hastings behind us and in flames,
we all lit up, even those of us who'd quit.

Fear of Fire

Don't ever call me scarface again, right.
Although we were the same size
he had me pinned against the wall
with a rage he'd been through fire to find.

I watched his face –
the tight smooth patch of skin
grafted on his forehead, the left eye
staring through crumpled tissue,
its lid drooped in the corner
as if smudged with a potter's thumb,
the cheek like wax, melted and re-set,
the webbed corner of his mouth
which always pulled a smile into a sneer.

I stood there stunned, surprised
to find myself the prey, slack with fear,
waiting for the bones of his fist
to re-connect me.

        Instead he turned,
and walked away
to leave me trembling and alone,
inside a shame I'd recognise
again and again, each time
I got my fingers burnt.

Her Father, Sharpener of Knives

Where is he leading me, she dreams,
    as they stumble together
        down the old grown-over track.

He'd say she's leading him
    where they all end up, his kind –
        considering their knives,

playing the pads of their thumbs
    on a whisper of edge, drawing blood
        or sharpening blunts on stone.

And the knife he's handed her
    she's never seen before,
        though it fits snug in her palm

between one callus and another
    as if she's sliced onions or cut
        chrysanthemums with it for years.

Its chipped pot handle bound with string
    means nothing to her. Heirloom
        or token of a life not lived?

She'd ask but already knows his answer –
    kitchen drawer stacked with danger,
        bone-deep jab in the washing-up.

It's her turn now to keep them sharp,
    carvers sheathed, parers
        and scrapers facing south,

and this knife of unknown ancestry
   she's wielding as they lead each other
      down to the bottom pasture

where a milling crowd of fathers
   makes a space, receives him.
      She leaves them to it, comparing scars.

From the Cabinet of Idioms

Up here in the word museum, language's revolving doors
propel me to the cabinet of idioms, four square in my way,
the glint and rust of well-worn tropes hugger mugger on their shelves.

The fig my father couldn't give turns out to be an ear of dried fruit
hardening in its skin, though the cuss the tinker threw my uncle's way
still shines like a brassy blade you'd cut your tongue on if you spoke it.

And they may be rare, my grandmother's hen's teeth, but someone
must have sown a flock's worth and brought them on with slurry
till they sprouted like tin soldiers, pikes and cudgels ready
for dragons, cockerels and anything that moved before first light.

There's a wax stub, pillared with candle sperm, reminding me of hours
holding a light to what I never could, like the brother I didn't have.
And a pale stone wears a coat of dried blood
where my mother wore the mounts of her palms to blisters.

The Blue

You wait for it

and it never comes. Whatever it is
it never comes when expected.

All your life you believe in it,
as if it were part of your life,
a part you've not reached yet.

All your life you prepare your life.
But how, you wonder, will it come.
Like a stubbed toe
or the shock from a dodgy switch;

or evening sun shuffling your shadow
as you walk in the woods? Like a phone call
when you're out; a sense of déjà vu
slipping like a plastic loid between
the lock and latch of conversation?

Perhaps in the marrow of the night
it'll slit your dreams, spilling them
like ticker tape; or one morning
you'll leave the house with a light step
and no inkling why.

And should the voice of a lost-touch lover
with a sceptical smile
and a way of saying your name
that turns old wounds in their scars

whisper a place and time
in your head, you'd go, after all,
just in case, believing

in something unreachable
reaching to touch you

out of it.

North Uist

You can't bring it home, the light.
It belongs to the sea, to crystals of salt
in the air, to white sand blown
through spikes of marram. It's what water
refuses, peaty lochans bending it back
from the steel blue shield
they hold to the sky. It's carried
like hidden elixir in the bellies of clouds,
in pellets of hail, the hatchmarks
of sleet in the air. It's carried
through prisms of droplets,
rainbows doubled, reversing the spectrum
then fading like a faint
after-image, as over your shoulder
a new squall musters its violets and blues.

The painter may reach for the brush
and the knife, compelled like a fiddler
by the tune turning round in her head.
And the canvas might glow
like a filled sail, its spillage of colours
a chart for imaginary landfall.
But it's not the work of the painter,
it's not the paint you can see:
wrap the canvas and carry it back
to the mainland, it's merely stretched weave
plastered with body and pigment.
Like a plant deprived of its native soil,
it jades on an inland wall.
Should you want to find your way back
this isn't the map you'll need.

Mack

Mack's from an island no one lives on any more.
    The ocean that offered them
    saithe, pollack, lobster, cod,
    now offers only the sound
    of itself on a bad landline
    and heartache – slight but persistent
    like a draught beneath a byre door.

Mack's a new man on a downtown island now.
    The roar of traffic's louder than the sea.
    He lives on a street full of islanders like him
    in and out of one another's houses,
    old words keeping the old world true
    while without their knowing it
    another language changes them.

Mack's a creel of memories.
    He hauls them to the surface if you ask
    but first he picks about. There's no
    helping yourself. It's his catch, his call.
    Sometimes he sorts a bad one out
    then throws it back before you've time
    for a glimpse of the truth it hides.

Mack's the future, Mack's the past.
    He takes things as he finds them, finds himself
    with no need for a compass, reading
    the sea of faces, the swell of voices
    fighting in his ears the way he'd read
    the spumey waves to bring the boat home,
    the way he reckoned the turning tide.

Nothing fazes Mack
    He drives a car with a fancy number plate.
    His children swear allegiance to perpetual youth,
    his son enlisting for its war, his daughter
    off to college. Neither know the words their parents
    call out in their sleep, nor the creeping melancholy
    fog brings from the sea.

Mack's at home a long long way from home.
    You can see it in the way he speaks two tongues,
    takes words from one to complement the other.
    You can see it in the way he leans
    into any wind, a forward stoop to keep his boots
    at a pushing angle to the ground.
    It's the way you tell an islander apart.

Atlantic Room

A westerly whistles through the gap
in a rotten window frame.

On the warped sill an urchin shell
keeled over on the bubbled
off-white gloss. Tweed curtains reek.

Somewhere out there
beyond the walled garden, rough-cut lawn,
neglected borders (iris, sea-kale, montbretia),

beyond the small hump of the graveyard
where headstones jostle
this way and that for a better view,

beyond the spirit-level of the horizon
lies America.

Last stop before Nantucket
announces the sign as we drive up.

The sea's moods play all day with ours.
Wet sands come and go. America
remains America:

invisible land of no return,
inviting the heart
                    to a change of heart,
leaving behind it
a hole a gale blows through.

Through the Blizzard a Man Walks
after Richard Long

He is in his element. He calls it art.
He will count the hours. He will call them art.
He will count the tors. He will call them art.
He will count his footsteps perhaps
as he plods through the white world,
lashes clagged with snow, imagination
spinning his compass. He will remember
himself as he once was, silent, alone
in the wide world of possibility.

He treads snow, half leans on the wind,
eyes watching grass bend, grit skid
on iced puddles. Through the white whirl
looms the land's knuckle, bare bone
in its plastering of snow, stone rampart,
castle, house shape, a whistling,
a sense of something arrived at.
Is it home? Or is it art?

A man walks through a blizzard.
He is not at home.
He is in his element.

Starship Mazda

I left the planet one night driving home
across the mid-Pennine watershed,
that road from Hebden Bridge to Oxenhope,
the slaloming tarmac trail across
soul-dark Wadsworth Moor, a spine of cat's-eyes
(how the car clung to the camber), chevrons
of reflective paint like ancient signs.

Where the road levelled and crested, the moor
breathed its peaty fog, body vapour
of some astral behemoth. Then clear again
and above me stars, ahead
the gold and orange nebulae of Haworth,
Keighley, Silsden hanging in space and time.

For two whole minutes I cruised on automatic
down the curling warp of the A6033,
suspending thoughts of reaching home –
a warm bath and companioned bed –
knowing this as home, this timeless drift
above an unearthed glittering spawn, miles
(or is it light-years?) off, a galaxy of streets and islands
I'd have to find a way through soon,
letting it, in its own way, pass through me
as I drove on west to join an earthbound self.

Flying Blind

'the happiness of the journeying hours'
Antoine de Saint-Exupery

I remember how we'd have no news
for weeks on end
before his silhouette pushed out against
the edges of the door.
And like a nomad he'd come in
to fill our house
with a cargo of unspoken thoughts.

I remember now the stonesweight
of foreboding.
Below the sea of clouds, he used to say,
lies eternity
and the riddle of his smile would bank
and turn to port
as if a brilliant point of light had caught his eye.

I remember how these homecomings
were like the past relived
or the future snatched back from itself,
his key in the door
worrying away at a welcome always hostage
to the heart's distraction,
a wing-light's glow on cloud,
the galaxy of instruments,
the fleshless vertebrae of mountains.

Timing

From the radio a bluesman plays clustered notes
with impeccable timing. A man with his
ordinary living – an old janitor perhaps,
entering an empty concert hall, shuffling onstage
to lift the piano lid and start boodling.

Imagine this music in that space, the resonance
of improvised chords, the pauses
trembling sometimes just long enough
to touch silence, the sound of hammered wire
singing to plush seats, drapes, ornate plasterwork;

the molecules in the air refigured into a spell
that would outlast the moment this
solitary player quietly closed the lid,
shuffled off-stage to resume his rounds,
checking windows, doors, air conditioning.

All those who'd come later, be it to hear
Beethoven or Benny Goodman, would know
as they found their seats and settled expectantly
that already there was something
important in their lives they'd missed.

As Is Our Custom

after Lawrence Durrell, Balthazar

We stop the clocks when guests arrive,
their stays so brief, their visits so rare.
Out here where the desert eats our fields,
we dine on solitude, hear mirrors talk.
The river's a twitching nerve at the end
of a long arm reaching for the heart.
News comes upstream in ripples, rumours
from the city we choose to live without.

When guests appear we know it as a sign.
We're reminded of ourselves, become
ourselves again, though words are strangers
stranger than our guests at first. Don't take it amiss
if we're curt or can't look you in the eye.
It takes so long to remember how to say
welcome, the house is yours; for truly
it's not ours to offer. We're guests ourselves,

as the ticking, chiming clocks affirm,
marking the moments, hours, the days
beyond counting, as if a lifetime were enough.
But the sun's parabola, the moon's moods,
the wind scattering our footprints
measure what most matters in the end: how glad
we are of visitors, their awkward ways
before our shy solicitudes, their innocent arrivals.

Reddleman

It was sometimes suggested that reddlemen were criminals for whose misdeeds other men had wrongfully suffered.
Thomas Hardy, *The Return of the Native*

You're woken at first light, sprawled
on the wreck of your bed, curtains still undrawn
from last night's drunken tumble.

You think you hear the creak of wheels, the tock
of hooves from an old sour nag. It's nothing
but a trade that died out centuries ago:

revenant, about the byways, farm to farm,
a figure dyed red, head to foot
and feeding rumour, how better men have hung

for what he's done. He makes his way
out of the way, along back lanes, the old drove road,
across the ford to the moor's wide berth.

A mutterer, they say, talking to himself.
Get close enough to listen and you've drawn too close.
So leave him to his died-out trade, he's history.

Leave him to the wind, its lack of concentration,
priorities elsewhere, or to the river,
its chokes and deadfalls, problems of its own.

At Five Lane Ends the gibbet of a signpost
has him stopped to scratch his head
before deciding east, or west, or north

or back again the way he came. It makes no odds.
You've woken early to the creak
of your own tall tale, that's all.

Lightning Calls

A single ring, always that,
like a misdial or second thoughts.
Humidity's so high the air
almost precipitates.

Must be lightning,
the line struck, stray volts
twitching the handset's stapes.
A yawn of static down the line,

the vacuum left
when someone says hallo
and no one answers. Perhaps
it wants to sell me something –

or even brag a bit: slashed trees,
roof slates flicked
like playing cards, computers
blown brainless.

I feel it getting personal,
a flashlight in the garden, scar-shape
peering through the shed
(those old illegal poisons).

It's mayhem's skinny dancer
closer than the devil.
Positive to negative
it earths itself. I feel it

like a touch of vertigo,
like being found out in a lie.

The Frog-eyed God of the Septic Tank

has a point to make which he always makes
when it's thunder or cutting rain
or the yard's a skirmish of black ice
or the summer air's so close you think
you'll drown if you inhale too fast;
always when we're somewhere else,
the shells of our bodies about the house
like androids, the mind unearthed,
scanning tomorrow or yesterday,
the blood's hydraulics ticking over
as we make beds, feed geese, fetch logs,
accounting for the day as if it's late already,
crossing our fingers that the goddess Sleep
will sleep with us tonight. We'll bank the fire,
check the back door's locked and trust
all this is enough to be going on with.

He'll make his point when it suits, shove
a three-fingered fist up the outfall,
jam the flush, burp blowback to announce
an underworld resentful of our ease.
See to it. See to it.

Local History

Some nights the valley's a river of children.
I hear their hopscotch and tag,
their movements shadowed by water,
its eddies, splashes, the all-of-a-sudden

silence a pool gives off like a sigh.
There's the jump of a shout like a fish
or a secret spilled in a panic of giggles,
cross your heart and hope to die.

Or there's a shriek; it could be a game
or it could be the girl whose father
would, years later, shoot himself
for reasons her mother couldn't explain.

And the two boys fighting are my neighbour
and the milkman, who'll both end up
the best of mates. I hear
their grunts and thumps as they labour

away at some family grudge
neither understands. And those twin sisters
who emigrated years ago, they're paddling
about on a raft their father's bodged

from plastic barrels and a broken gate.
Yes, there are children here who'll carry
the valley with them like a faith;
and others the river still holds in their place.

I listen as voices leapfrog away upriver,
a weave of echoes called back home
where a gutter sings in the peat,
moorland rain trickles through heather.

Digging
After Jane Routh, *Trace*

You're in two worlds at once:
beside me, watching the beck, its old ice
and dead leaves stacked like books

and with the long-dead, never-met
who lived here centuries ago
and left their traces, not in books

but in snowdrops, fragments
of clay pipe and earthenware
in the worked soil of the vegetable plot.

What you're telling me is made up,
made up as in 'the truth',
piecing together hard lives, purposeful:

the miner in the bell-pit,
his wife's toil to the common well,
their many children.

You imagine how they'd feel today,
alarmed and disbelieving,
the mines collapsed or infilled,

woods silent – no sound of saw,
billhook or cleaver, the hazel coppice
just mossy clumps the deer graze.

We must be their worst nightmare,
the future's ghosts hovering among them
in their cramped cottage.

By the light of a tallow lamp
he reads aloud – Psalms or Ecclesiastes,
she mends

and upstairs the children sleep
the sleep of the loved
who frequently go hungry.

What they've left us you're decoding now,
your head a world turned over
like good-hearted soil to yield

the whereabouts of old shafts,
the miner's route to work, their church,
the corner of the field she kept her hens.

So we stand by the beck
and you're centuries away.
I'm squinting through the present,

bare ash and their bars of shadow,
looking for our future's ghosts.
What is it we'll leave them?

Easier to guess what it is
we'll leave each other –
unread books, our *shapen clothes*.

Fine-tuned

Dusk. Kitchen. On the table his third cup
cools. It's been a long story. Sixty years.
A figure in a meadow, still as a scarecrow,
barrel down, safety off, watching, listening.

Sixty years. Six hundred moles a year.
Thirty six thousand and still
volcanoes of subsoil on the lawn,
catacombs beneath the meadow.

Give him his time back, he'd do it again,
all those motionless hours,
the world's sounds, wrensong, buzz,
the parting of grass, flitch of a twig;

how the day's moods season him –
dusk, for instance, with its owls.
No natural enemies, he says,
they'll talk to you – like this –

and from his pocket he draws
an empty shellcase, slips it
between first and second finger, squeezes,
blows. Owlsound fills the house.

An answer brings the woods indoors.
When he's gone we take it in turns
with the empty case. Nothing
but the coarse tuneless passage of air.

For a week we try, but it's too much
like teaching yourself to whistle
all over again,
just so you can join the gang.

Sootfall and a Cracked Mantlepiece

There's something about it, the hefting
and slotting of each log, settled and snug,
like building a wall from timber and air,
ends canted with straights so the whole stack
won't slither apart as it dries and shrinks
through summer's warm draughts, bark lifting
like antique leather, hearts splitting in spokes.

When it's finished and done, how you wish it were not.
You want more of the weighing and wedging,
the musk of cut alder, the sweet whiff of cherry,
the powder of sawdust clung to the hairs on your arms;
want more of the warmth of a good winter sweat
to exchange for next winter's glow from the hearth.
But step back to look and behold – a work of art
friends might admire or neighbours covet.

So who can blame Jamie? Mad as spooked stirks
he may be with his halo of hair like a dandelion clock,
but if you found the stack you'd not started to burn
depleted each day by an armful or two,
you'd dream something up – tell me you wouldn't.

Top of the pile there's a stout elm log. Imagine
drilling a hole (a 5/8ths bit, let's say), pouring in
the powder from a 12 bore shell, tamping it down,
inserting a plug (whittled dowel or cardboard wad),
slotting the log back exactly where you found it,
whistling to yourself some tell-tale off-key tune.

The Attic Fox

Never seen, but heard on lunar nights,
a softly softly trip of padded feet,
a scrape that goes with something in your dream.
So pull the hatch down, mount the ladder, shine a torch
through draughts and powdered plaster. They say
an attic's like a head. Well this one's empty,
cleared out months ago, ghostless and ingenuous.
Its smell's whatever's on the wind – snow,
slurry, cherry blossom.
                        The valve in the header tank
may drip from time to time, a moody
answer to the silence. A piece of gaffer tape,
used to fix an old light flex, whispers
when we brush it. And shadows in the eaves
jaywalk nimbly round the torchbeam. But no,
there's nothing here
                    and yet,
                            and yet, that smell –
it comes towards you sideways, sudden, sharp,
hot, foxy and is gone. In the truss of torchlight,
up through ruffled air, flecks of goosedown drift
like seeds of superstition, small wings
take flight in your belly, stick in your gullet
as you step back down the ladder, part sceptic, part not,
the cistern breaking into song for no good reason.

The Noise of Looking

We're leaning on the old bridge
     looking down at sky the river throws us glimpses of
between the flicker of new leaves
and sunlight like strips of torn foil trapped between rocks.

We're not talking much. The world's articulate enough.
Someone puts a finger to lips and points.
Even for those born here
     the commonplace can startle –
a grazing deer in the shade of a beech,
     its stare, the alert of its ears,
young antlers like early shoots of a stumpy plant.

It doesn't move and nor do we
     though we're the lesser before those eyes,
nostrils flaring for our scent.
Intruders, we watch,
     our attention taut as the deer's.
The first of us to move might break a spell, turn to stone
or fall to the ground gabbling the river's tongues.

But it's the deer moves first, dips its head to resume grazing.
We're an illusion, letting out breath, scuffing feet,
     turning,
leaving behind us the several ways a held gaze
     works on the mind, the moment and its memory.
When we look back the deer's watching us again, alarmed
and ready to bolt.

Rosie

There's a stirk fallen from the cliff
to the shelf of bedrock by the river.
The smashed contraption of its body
bleeds a little, one eye stares at the sky
with a look of almost surprise.
Already it stinks.

The land's too steep for a tractor,
the carcass too heavy for the few of us,
so you bring down Rosie from the luxury
of easy grazing. Your pleasure
at finding her work seems matched
by something in her gait,
the shiver of her flanks, the bob and shake
of her head as you fix the collar.

We tie the rope-ends to the beast's legs
and Rosie pulls, hooves gouging
steep peaty ground, an eagerness
you have to check so the deadweight
comes up evenly, doesn't snag
on an overhanging branch or swing
lop-sided under a rocky sill,
but eases gently over the cliff's lip.

You let her have her way then
and I'm that close I can recall even now
the piss and oatmeal smell,
those sweating buttocks, the pistons of her legs,
the startling energy of life at work
pulling its counterweight uphill.

Gift Horses

Some beasts anyone can mount and not fall off,
even bareback. They take you where you will.
No leggy thoroughbreds of course, skittish
fence-chewers, nothing with a price on its head;

more the traveller's painted mare
or the snigging pony, horse sweat and a halo
of flies round twitching ears, or the arthritic
gelding put back out to graze the fells.

But feed any one of them and those black
rubber lips rear up to reveal yellow megaliths
set in a slime of chewed grass, the rare steak
of a tongue, dappled with its lichen of lies,

pink lies, purple lies, black lies, lies so fat
and eloquent you're swallowed alive
to crouch in the belch of a barrelled belly
clutching your shield and imagining Troy.

A Trojan Poacher

I'd slip past the city guards at night,
   an ear tuned for the bailiff, his tread
      along the bank, the mutter

of his prayers, splash of his oblations –
   a coin here, a stolen bracelet there
      to keep the river god sweet.

But now when I part the rushes I wade
   shin-deep in mud and offal,
      shoals of limbs, bodies hacked

from their carapace of armour,
   broken blades, split shields,
      a blood-brown glow on moonlit water.

It's what comes from not being able to think
   above the clamour of the gods,
      their taunts and fickle loyalties.

It's what comes from thinking yourself
   immortal, like Achilles
      with his bad breath, bloodlust, boasts.

So were I a god I'd steal a march
   on whatever fate awaits him,
      wear a serpent's skin,

disguise myself as an alder root,
   bite him on the heel,
      fang to bone, venom to blood,

not letting go until the dead
   washed out to sea, their crusting armour
      treasure on the ocean bed.

Heads
  for Martin Copley

Head beside me. Paperweight.
Holding down its pillow of bills.
Raku skin, milky glaze,
a mouth still struggling
to pronounce its name.

Head on a plate. Veiled dance.
A whetted appetite.
Who'd spurn his queen.
Who'd be the executioner.
Curse the fool who weeps.

Head on a stake. Traitors gate.
An English betrayal. The barge
brings in successions.
Love impaled.
Counsellor. Queen. None escapes.

Head in the sand. Listen. An army,
advancing, retreating, whatever.
Or the whisper of no one
absolutely no one
for miles.

Head in the clouds.
Swaddled in dreams.
Blue sky thinking in a storm.
Hollow heart
in a whistling cage.

Head in your hands. A weight
off your shoulders.
A great relief to finger
the dents, the bumps
of your grief.

Head on a plinth. Marble eyes,
pupil-less, a Homer, making it up,
insisting the truth is only the truth.
Remember, remember
to spit out the pit.

Head in a field.
Deaf ear to the ground.
No memory of pike or blade.
Buried, bleached,
turned by the plough like a tuber.

Speak. Speak.

Theseus with Post Traumatic Stress

He dreams he's in hospital in a foreign language.
His heart is fluent in the varied tongues of power
but for once he chooses to wait for the doctor,
her tear-stained cheeks, her gift for interpretation.

He sleepwalks down a white and echoing labyrinth.
He is without a ship, without a compass,
without a ball of string, obedient to plastic signs,
their two-way arrows as he searches for a payphone.

Through the receiver he picks up heavy breathing,
hooves on cobble setting his teeth on edge,
inconsolable weeping, the flapping robes of a body
falling to the sea. He slams it back in its cradle

and a bell rings in his brain. He wakes up
imagining he's cured. The doctor takes his pulse,
squints into the distance, catches her breath
at the sight of a black sail beckoning mistakenly.

There's a fist of pain behind his sternum
like a bruise where once he'd beaten on his chest
to call down gods, their gangland muggings,
arbitrary heroes, shifty moves in complicated games.

How he'd like to explain, if only the doctor would listen,
if only he could find the words, his old edgy spiel,
but in the ginnels of his skull a new voice limps,
first person still, alone but not so singular.

A Day Out With The Neuro-surgeon

I came round in an arctic shiver, limbs
convulsing like a puppet's. On the half hour
a pen torch in my eyes, questions:
my name, what year is it, where am I?

Brown fluid draining from the skull,
a saline drip, a catheter, at every turn
a knot of tubes and lines,
but still I know my name, the date, the time.

The patient opposite me mirrors something else,
white dressing on his skull from ear to ear.
I watch him spooning ice cream in his soup,
see the dark stain when the sheets are changed.

I tell myself I'll soon be gone. Air miles
and passport in the bag. No shit on my pyjamas,
just a small hole in the head, and two titanium screws
the boarding gate detector won't pick up.

Beneath the sheets my fingers cross, uncross,
like scissors from a car-boot sale, too blunt to cut.

The Four Houses

I was born in a house of weapons, the dank yawn
of its hallway, walls hung with mayhem:
rapier, broadsword, axe, shillalegh, mace and pike.
Or the blood-tang in the gun room, glint
of a spent cartridge, crosshair shadows in the attic.

I was weaned in a house of words. They swaddled me,
coddled me, stood me up, cut me down to size,
coaxed me through my first steps, let me fall.
I stood back up alone, learned to pit my weight against
sweet nothings, blunt truths, needle-sharp insinuations.

I was trained in a house of mirrors. Everywhere I went
the world I saw saw through me. My lack reflected back
from every angle. So I learnt disguise, the beard,
camouflage of confidence, smoke screen smiles, the frown's
parry, the slight shake of the head – is that yes or is it no?

I live in a house of companionship. The game of chance
is played out here. It brings me to my senses.
What there is to learn I learn from others. We rub along
under the same roof, its sniper's attic, obsolete
accoutrements, tricksy mirrors, armouries of words.

The Illegal Immigrant in the Red Jumper

I found him practising my signature. *One day* he explained *I might want to buy a blue leather sofa.* (We'd been window shopping.) *Red and blue don't go I told him.*

He got a job when I wasn't looking. I saw the red jumper carrying a hod six storeys up. That night I demanded rent, danger money. But how do you take money from a man who'd spent ten hours in a baggage hold?

You'll have to remove that jumper I said. *You stick out a mile.* He shook his head. It was knitted by his sister and reminded him of home.

I hid him in the attic. My wife caught him sneaking back from the kitchen with a handful of flapjacks. *I told you to keep out of sight* I hissed, as she shoved him out the back door.

He took off the red jumper, folded it ceremoniously like a flag from a soldier's coffin, then presented it as if we were next of kin. From his eyes spilled the airless dark of a container truck.

Prospect Street

In this age of backpacks, sling sacks,
shoulder and bum bags, how strange
to meet a man with a suitcase.

Not one of those designer jobs
with telescopic handles and trolley wheels,
but old-fashioned pulpboard,

its veneer of brown plastic
peeling at the corners, tinny handles
and spring locks lacquered to seem like brass.

It had a look about it of the new world,
crowds disembarked onto a jostling quay,
or the old one

where it might have lain with all the others,
hurled into a windowless room
or down a dead-end corridor.

But he was young, this new immigrant, the age
I might have been when I bought my first
rucksack and had those dreams.

He asked the way,
showed me a scrap of paper, an address
in a script as laboured as his accent.

But I shook my head, explained
I'd lived here all my life
and hadn't heard of Prospect Street.

From the look on his face it was hard to tell
if he didn't get a word I was saying,
or simply didn't believe me.

Fugitive

Each night I sleep in a different house,
a rich man's divan or an old crone's
sacking on a lino floor. Each night
it's prayers to a different god, food
for an alien soul. But each night
it's the same dream. I'm flying
above a city that goes on forever.
I look down on side-streets and alleys,
snickets and shortcuts at figures
running this way and that, glancing back
over shoulders and crouching to hide
at a cough or footsteps or snatches of talk.
And just as I wake, it's always the same,
they're my friends, the friends
I grew up with. For Alice and Louis,
Isaac, Ahmed and Hans, trying to reach
a safe house to dream in, I hold my breath
and pray to a different god each night.

Language Problem

They sit me in front of a camera,
give me a script.

There's a language problem.

Where I come from, I try to explain,
a word can have many meanings.
They don't seem to hear.

My government, I insist,
only does business with big business.

There's a language problem.

Under their masks I can tell
things aren't going well. I look
into eyes with no faces and listen.

Terms of endearment in one tongue
can be expletives in the other.
I am not good at translation.

The word for dream, I get that.
The word for god and, I think, blood
and prize, or is it price?

Back home the man negotiating on the phone
is tongue-tied.
I need them to understand this,

how he's locked inside a room
with taped-up windows and a television
showing old and future wars.
He is not important.

I read their script to the camera. Words
crumble in my mouth.

They play the video back to me.
I try to make what I say
mean what I want it to mean.

Diplomacy

Word is they're talking. But armies don't talk.
They mutter, they grumble, they seethe.
We've had it to here, stood to in dug-outs and rubble,
the sweat of the day, the bone cold frost of each night,
a platoon of duckers and divers in the other side's sights.

And stood down in the camp, all the briefings and drill,
the press-ups and card games, what does it come to?
It comes to a point when letters from home cut you off,
when hearts and kisses aren't matched by the words on the page,
when your daughter's drawings are maps of intrigue

and your wife someone else's, someone you no longer are,
a skin of a former self shed in a season
of snatched sleep and squints through the green glare
of nightsights, your homesick and half-awake mind half-
tuned to the guy to your right, his black jokes, faraway heart.

The Summit

The place was a crumbling bungalow, some old-timer's
holiday haunt, walls now pocked by shrapnel and bullets.

He came out to meet us, all smile and guile, proffered his left hand,
his right held up to display the stub of thumb and index.
A gift, he said, to God, then steered me inside.

Two lumpy chairs, rum in black tea brewed on a primus,
a driftwood fire and local radio floating through from the kitchen
where our aides sat it out playing blackjack for matchsticks.

His quick boyish grin, the bone of a smile in my throat.
A bad joke we both laughed at too loud. Then it was business:
exits bolted and sealed, armed guards round the back;

the cut and the deal, not playing it too close to your chest,
not showing your hand; the saving of face by risking your neck.

No Mention in Dispatches

The fridge behind, humming to itself
like a bored and tone-deaf sentry,
the slap of cards on an old ammo box,
poker-faced voices raising, seeing,
the scratch of a biro writing home.

An off-duty night and he's sprawled
on his bunk, remembering
the kitchen at home, the electric clock
with its artificial tick – another sound
you only hear when you stop.

What came next was one-off,
dead-of-night, a stray round looking
for a life to trash, a noise so big it left
no room inside him, not in his bones,
his brains, not in the miles of his gut.

But the fridge took the blast. Stood to
between them and the perimeter it burst
like a winded beast, spitting yoghurt
and shrapnel. They ran, grabbing gear,
the night hysterical with small-arms fire,

to be met by medics with stretchers
and body bags. But the only casualty
was the Queen of Clubs and a scratch
from a splinter of biro. Two weeks later,
tour over, they were flying.

To see them today, you'd never guess
the hidden mark on each left shoulder –
'Zanussi'. His wife can't stand tattoos
but better this she has to admit,
than roses and an arrow through the heart.

The Gift of Words

They jump from his mouth,
        obscenities,
mid-conversation, a propos
        of nothing but themselves,
gratuitous, vandals
        from a black logic.

In court he's hunched,
        wishing himself invisible,
desperate to choke them back
        swallow their stones. The floor
possesses his stare. His hands
        attack themselves like ferrets.

Unwittingly he makes the case
        for his defence.
CUNT. The clerk's mouth
        struggles with a smile.
BOLLOCKS. The young brief
        waiting for the next case
giggles. The chairwoman's eyebrows
        dip beneath a steel rinse.
At the back his mother's hanky
        shakes in her hand.

They give it a name of course,
        a syndrome nobody
can understand, but labelled
        demons feel no shame.
The words are always there
        to punch you
where you listen,
        where you care.

If you can choose yours
            spare a moment SHITFACE
to consider the gift of words
            we offer one another.

Keys

There are five of them. They hang
from their chain like the fingers
of a smashed hand,
divining bones.

They open gates, heavy-hinged doors,
or lock the day down,
slammed answer
to a question out of place.

The long chain swings from my waist.
I'm a key-slave shackled to their spell.
Nagged by gravity
they wear my pocket thin.

Sometimes I'll reach a gate to hoik out
this mesh of metal shanks,
their bits jammed in a knot of links
I have to shake free like a shaman's rattle.

Beyond the bars a shadow in a recess shifts.
Let us through boss?
A dash, a skirl of dust,
a sparrow on the gym roof.

Life

I'd say he was at sea. If only, my mother said,
giving me the sort of look grown-ups give grown-ups.

I'd say he worked on the rigs, the Gulf of Mexico.
The kid two doors along confided his was in Bolivia.

I'd say nothing of the monthly trips, gates and doors,
the hubbub of a long room, formica table-tops, plastic cups.

For a man who claimed he hadn't meant to, he smiled a lot,
more often and wider as the years went by.

For a man who didn't know when, he kept up with the news,
read between the lines, worked out his answers.

For a man lost to the innocence of words, he left it to his smile
to see him through – goodbyes, Christmases, divorce.

For a man who finally got out, what he likes best now
is staying in. From his seventh floor flat the town's unchanged.

He keeps a tally of my visits; we share a takeaway,
a game of chess I always lose, the comfort of long silences,

though when I ring the bell and listen as he slides the bolt,
rattles the chain, there's a familiar urge to run

before the front door opens and we're both giving it that
kite-wide, wouldn't-harm-a-fly, killer of a smile.

Thin Air

His file was a lure of failed appointments
like a scent dragged over a hound-trail.
I rapped on his kick-scuffed door, unannounced
(always a risk with a marked man).
The door was opened by the girl he called his
'wee wife' – a girl I'd known as the wee wife
of Bob Barney before his current stretch
for holding a blade to a taxi-driver.
She wore a negligee and sipped at a cocktail glass
complete with umbrella. It was midday.
Tommy tripped on his way downstairs –
an Ulster curse, untucked shirt, the smell of sex
and perfume and that smoke and mirrors charm
with which he'd given both sides the slip back home.

Ah, Mr B, come in, come in. Pina colada?
But a ménage à trois was no setting for the riot act,
delivered with my usual pussy-footed eloquence,
direct threats and sweet reason
cancelling each other in the same breath.
His wee wife giggled while Tommy wore
his armour-plated smile. At least he was alive.
At least we'd both gone through the motions.
Next time I called, of course, he'd gone.
There's money on it the warrant's still a curled
and yellowing sheet on an unmanned desk.
I wish them well, Tommy and Bob Barney's
ex-wee wife. May they thrive on the thin air
they have to breathe to keep two steps ahead.

Policeman's Heel

*Plantar Fasciitis: an inflammation of the ligament connecting
heel and toes, caused by standing or walking on hard surfaces for
long periods.*

There's a lurch to his stride as if one step's in the gutter.
He's a lame dog following the scent of a crime,

stalker of second guesses, cross-examiner of lamplight,
hedge-twitch, the muffled reports of car doors.

He's out there everyone knows, lonely old nosey old
shadow, putting together the day's two and two's

and getting the answer he wants. And what does he know
as he stands on the corner looking both ways,

easing the weight off one leg? Between the quiet
of the missing and the soap of a neighbour's din,

between a sudden nicking and a cry for help,
there's only the pounding of miles, the noting of names,

graffiti, car numbers, the old church stripped of its lead,
the dark slots of half-opened doors half-closing.

A 5.00 am wake-up

The front door flew open, splintering the jamb.
Hands in the air, we came downstairs to find the wind
rushing from corner to corner, room to room
like a pack of sniffer dogs. Back in the kitchen
the invisible bulk of their handler stumbled and wheezed.

Out in the street footsteps ran in all directions, car alarms
brayed, milk bottles rolled like comics splitting their sides
at a bad joke. The body I'd been burying in my dream
followed me about, miming step for step.

And you, of course, couldn't see it, having had no hand
in the deed. Resigned to days of cleaning up, you saw
a freak of nature, act of God, insurance get-out. I read it all
as omen: how some night or day or ungodly hour's
ram-raiding storm I'd finally be caught red-handed.

Manna

As rumour follows storm, word got round:
a freighter grounded, crated cargo
washed up and ours for the picking.
A wheelbarrow stacked to tottering height
with surgical gloves and shower caps,
then a boy from the Creek estate
wheeling a silver Kawasaki up the street,
frame and two wheels, no tank. A neighbour
handed out bird tables, survival equipment
should we at last be driven to a diet
of finches and robins. Ironing boards, televisions,
kites, ornamental garden barrels. Cookery books.

Lorry loads. The coming and going.
Where from, where to, a mystery.
Our bypassed town with its silted harbour,
its quarrymen on half time, a sudden Klondike,
all night traffic of traffickers, an invasion
of transits, trailers, trucks and cattle boxes,
the shed skins of fast food littering
gutters, choking drains. We're a hungry town
at the end of the day, at the end of the line,
but as St Peter might have said to the couple
going nowhere, their pick-up axle deep in shingle,
there's only so much you can do
with fifteen 20 metre rolls of deckchair fabric.

The Bus Shelter at Road End
after the Unst Bus Shelter

Any further and you meet the North Atlantic,
its grey spume, its slap in the face. Turn round,
look south, everywhere you've been already

and beyond. Is this what you want?
Knowing the way home, waiting
for a bus you hope will never get here.

There's a faux leopardskin easychair and a pile
of National Geographic on a seventies
coffee table with wonky screw-on legs.

You can read while you wait, other lives:
Tibetan nomads, faces smeared with yak grease
against a cold that turns prayer brittle;

the homebound miner, shift-snagged and spooked
by daylight; or the wire-man leaning
above the swell, fingers on the fathoms' pulse.

You can have it all ways here. The skeech
of an onshore wind, the comfort of home, of sorts,
plastic daffodils, net curtain, visitor's book.

You sit with your back to the sea.
But it goes on making its noise in your ear,
unbearable distance, unbearably near.

The Lost Days

I have memories of thaw,
    your voice in a field of cloud.
I have memories of flood,
    brown water's twist and splice,
games rooks play on the wind
    as it barges through the valley
like a thief chased by dogs.

I have a voice intoning
    in the chancel of my brain.
It says the same thing
    over and over. It could be Latin,
it could be code,
    or it could be a scrambled message
on the ansaphone. And then
    there's sunlight through stained glass,
its see-through throw of colours
    like a miracle spilt on a tomb.

I have a museum of scrimshaw,
    harpoons, kayaks and eskimo masks,
whalers trapped in ice,
    a container ship rounding Spurn Head
as we lunch on a gun-emplacement
    peering across at Cleethorpes.
I have the sound of the car and a bus
    colliding, the complexity
of one-way systems,
    bruised edges of the day.

I have pockets of sweet wrappers,
    tickets, debit card receipts.
I pull out my hand
    and they drop to the ground
or scud downwind, their coded clues
    a forensic geek with a taste
for a paper chase might use
    to access my bank account,
birthplace, dna, actuarial death.
    But the days themselves are lost data.

Holding the Door

I held the door for my daughter
who waved and disappeared
before I'd had a chance to smile.
I held the door for my grandmother
still ramming her trolley
against the heels of the person ahead.
I held the door for a couple arguing,
I knew their words by heart.
I held the door for a pair of trainers
and a tiny muscular dog which sniffed my toes.
I held the door for a scar of scarlet lipstick
pursed in permanent disapproval.

I held the door for the verb 'to love'
declining itself endlessly
to strobe lights and a drum machine;
for the colour red, it wore a mini-skirt
on a pale exhausted body;
for faith, looking straight ahead,
eyes fixed on the vanishing point;
for famine, trying to explain itself
again and again with the sound turned down;
for silence, its white sheet smoothed
and tucked into crisp hospital corners.

I held the door for childhood.
It flickered like an old newsreel
played in the daylight.
I held the door for history.
It swung through with a funny walk,
a punter in a hall of mirrors.
I held the door for tomorrow.
Blind fingers felt the furrows
on my brow, the creases down my cheeks.
I held the door for my shadow
but it seemed reluctant to go in front.

Footage

Pink Floyd, McCartney, Daltrey
thrashing their ghosts for charity.
And how we remember.
How the pledges pour in.

(how the ghosts inside us all
    tap their feet,
        click their bones)

Where do they go to,
the ghosts on the screen,
the famous, the famished,
the vanquished, the vanished?

(ghosts like family, intimate
    and inescapable, everyone
        we've been or might have been)

Where do they go
the anonymous ghosts
in their makeshift camps,
their crammed unseaworthy boats?

(waving our souvenir tickets,
    waving our arms
        slightly out of time)

Where does it go, the glitter,
the glamour, the jumping jack
flash of goodwill, the scaffolded stage,
the sea of lit faces, the patter?

(getting the song's off-by-heart words
    wrong but undeterred,
        in our heads and out of them)

Where do they go, the litter, the flies,
the stick-thin limbs, the queues
in a drought for water? Where does it go,
the news-crew's worn-through footage?

The Dance
after Edvard Munch

There's a dance done at sunset. By two girls.
It involves the sea, quiet waves embracing rocks,
the mantra of slip and suck, the beach
flushed pink in the sinking light, and the sun
on the water pointing a red finger their way
like an admonition, while two dark bystanders
shuffle about as if to a music they know is there
but can't hear above the small rattle of pebbles,
the scuff of feet in the sand as two girls whirl,
each taking the other's weight on the turn,
each flung round the other's orbit.

Just wait till the music stops the dark figures think
to themselves and the louring shoreline trees suggest
...but of course the music doesn't.
When the two girls tire and embrace to walk home
arm in arm, the music no one else can hear
stays with them. It plays like an endless coda,
a reel or jig the blood pumps out. It plays like life's
long friendship, a wedding feast, a child's birth cries.
It plays like envy's shadow, loss, the frenzy of a wake.
It plays to memory, fast and loose. It plays
straight-laced and close to its chest. It plays, it plays.

To the dark bystanders who can't hear
and never will, it mimics silence. To the louring trees
it plays a shaking wind. To the wind
it plays like sycamore or pines. To the sea
it plays pebbles, to sand it plays
like footsteps. To the sun it plays reflection,
to the long red finger of sunset
pointing across the waves it plays two girls,
elbows hooked as they spin one round the other.
To the girls it plays without a care.
There's a dance they do and this is how it goes.

73